Rosie Goodwin & Alice Chadwick

Splendid Cities

COLOR YOUR WAY TO CALM

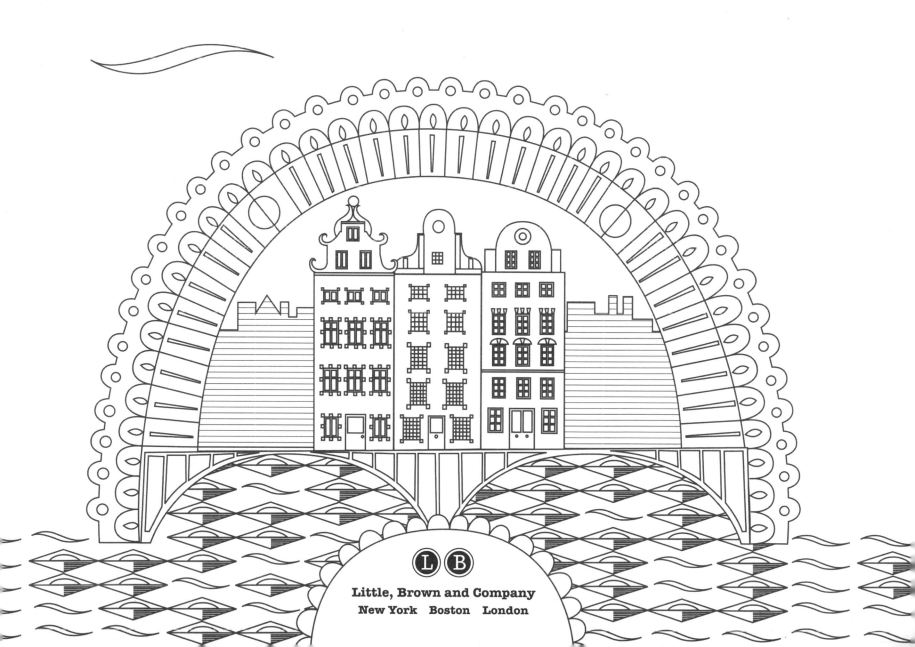

LB

Little, Brown and Company

New York Boston London

Little, Brown and Company
Hachette Book Group
1290 Avenue of the Americas, New York, NY 10104
littlebrown.com

First North American Edition: June 2015
Originally published as *Cités Merveilleuses* in France by Éditions Marabout, October 2014

Little, Brown and Company is a division of Hachette Book Group, Inc.
The Little, Brown name and logo are trademarks of Hachette Book Group, Inc.

The publisher is not responsible for websites (or their content) that are not owned by the publisher.

The Hachette Speakers Bureau provides a wide range of authors for speaking events. To find out more, go to hachettespeakersbureau.com or call (866) 376-6591.

ISBN 978-0-316-26581-2
Library of Congress Control Number: 2015938245

10 9 8 7 6

WW

Printed in the United States of America

Many thanks to Emmanuel, Catie, and Alice for allowing us to create this book. With special mention to Tom and Alba, Mum and Dad.
R. G.

Many thanks to Emmanuel and Catie, to Rosie for her inspired work and, as ever, to S, G & P—next summer we will discover a new place!
A. C.

Rosie Goodwin lives and works in East London. Her work in film and media is inspired by her London walks and her more distant travels.

Alice Chadwick is an illustrator who lives and works in East London. Her work appears in newspapers, magazines, books, and fashion.

These cities, real and imagined, were brought to life by:

....

★ Find:

1 pod of dolphins

9 fish

2 sea lions

6 jellyfish

1 pair of turtledoves

6 butterflies

1 flock of geese   4 swans

2 chickens

1 stork   7 birds

6 goldfish

2 seahorses

2 phoenixes

1 pair of pigeons

2 sparrows

1 robin

1 flock of ducks

1 owl

1 pelican   1 parrot

1 peacock

1 crow

5 whales

2 ostriches

1 pack of grouse

1 seagull

3 pigeons

2 toucans

4 flamingos

3 wrens

3 bats

1 swarm of bees

5 flying fish

2 sharks

2 eagles

3 birds perching

Other cities and towns — some real, some imaginary — are just waiting for you to bring them to life:
San Francisco, Bombay, Istanbul, Sydney, Moscow, Granada, London, Montreal, Tokyo, Amsterdam, Stockholm, Paris, Rio de Janeiro, and Mexico City.

Welcome to our dream cities...

The pages of this book will take you on a journey around the world that includes floating kingdoms and phantasmagorical cities. The sky is the limit, with each picture hiding a treasure trove of surprises. Let these cities cast their enchanting spell upon you.

Along your way you will encounter many traveling companions who will accompany you by air or water as you bring these pages to life. Look carefully for a pod of dolphins, a smack of jellyfish, or a swarm of bees.

Take your time, relax, de-stress, and give your imagination free rein. Armed with your pencils and felt tip pens, you will discover the calming and creative pleasures of coloring in.

Bon voyage!

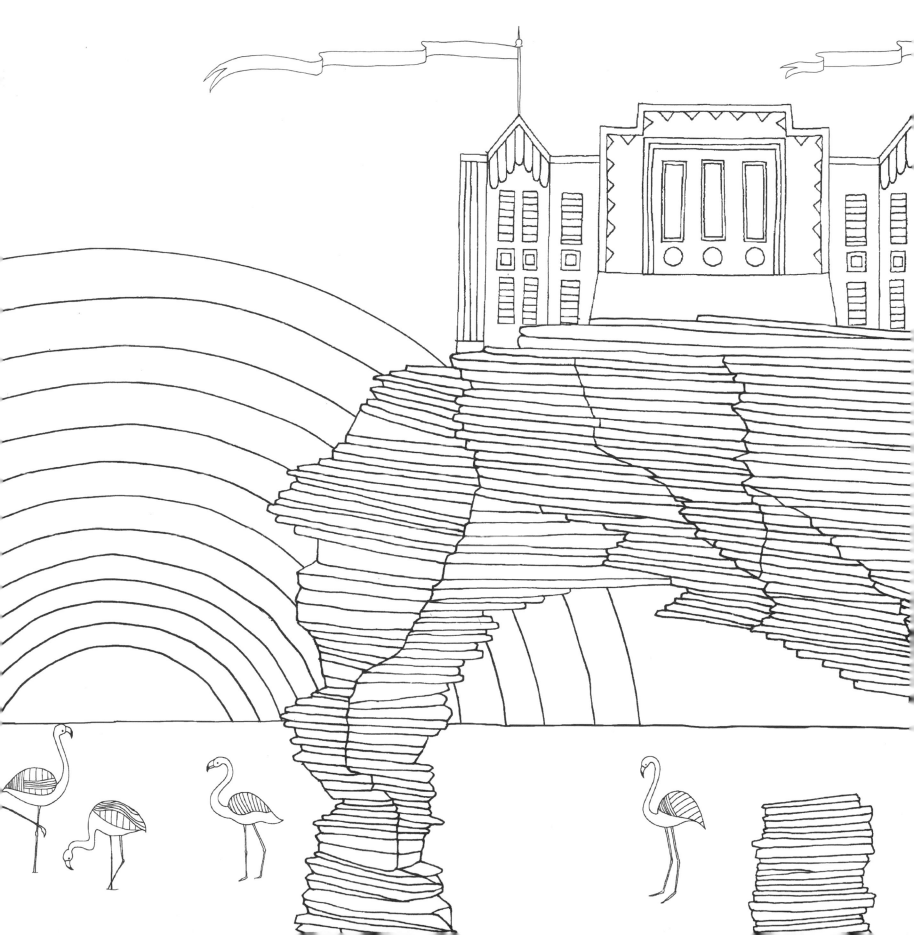

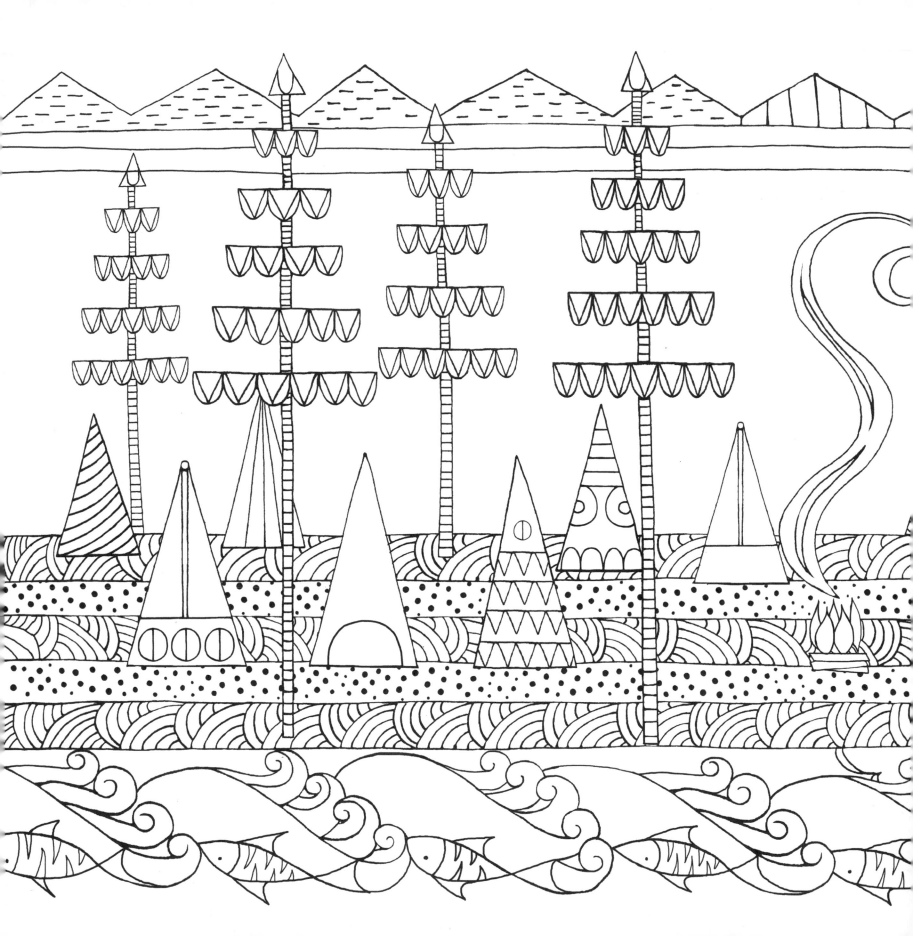

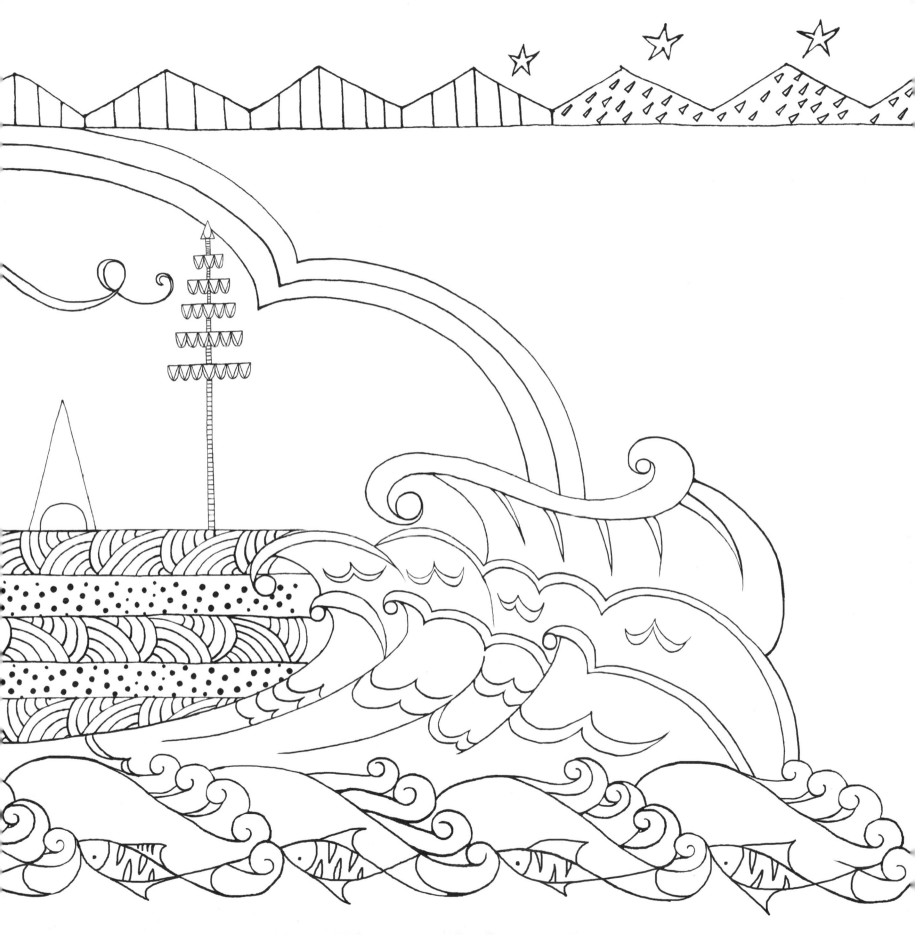

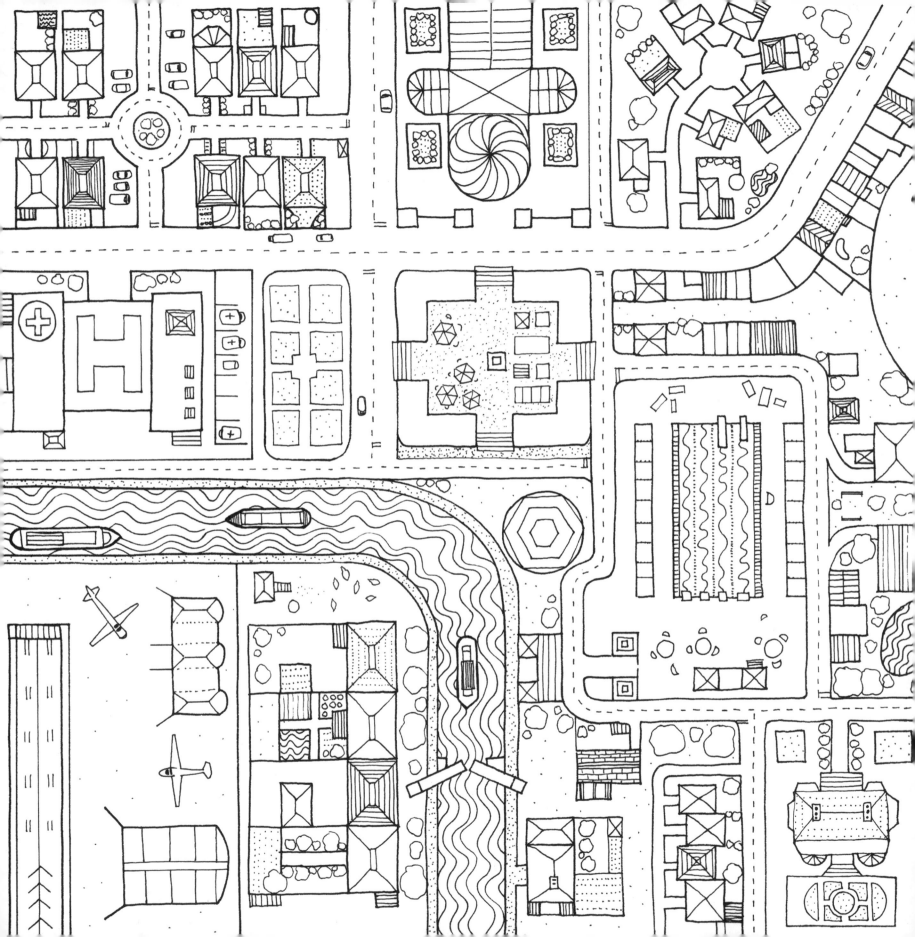

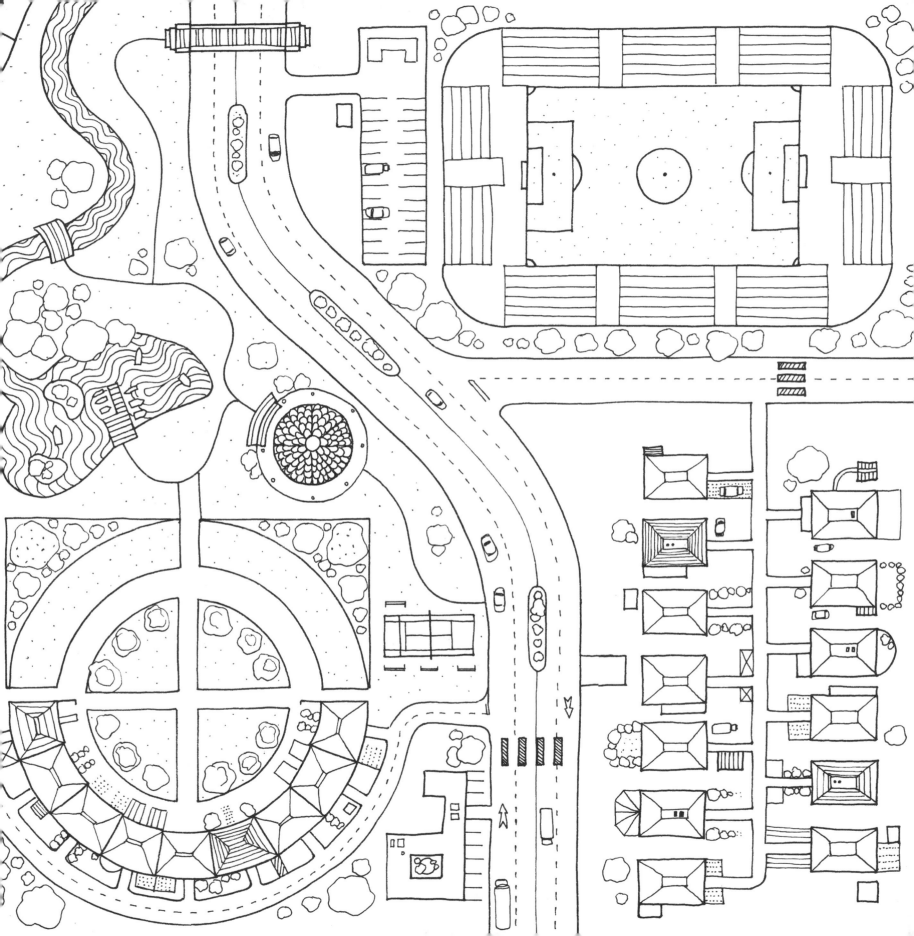

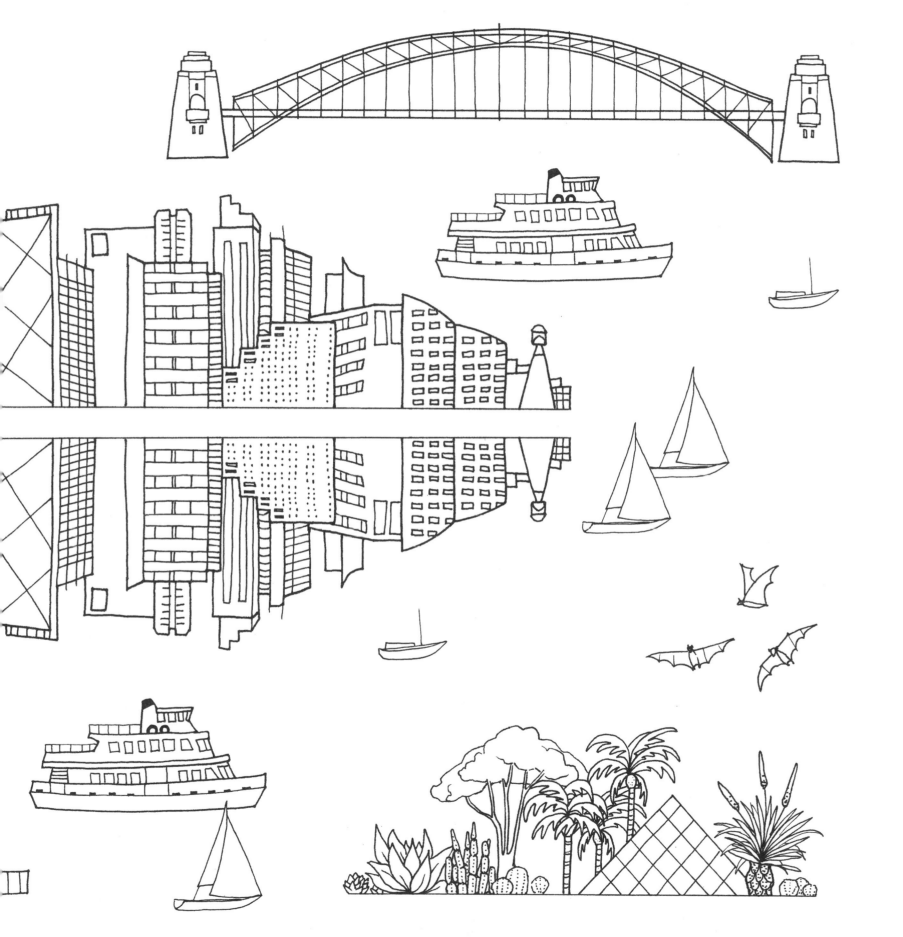

Answers:

A fantasy kingdom: 1 pod of dolphins

Paris: 1 pair of turtledoves

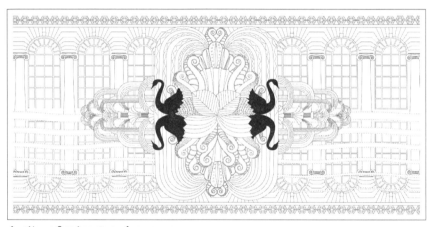

A city of mirages: 4 swans

On the rooftops: 1 seagull

A city of stone: 4 flamingos

A funfair: 2 birds

An enchanted world: 2 seahorses

Amsterdam: 1 stork

A medieval city: 2 chickens

Stockholm: 1 flock of geese

Art deco: 1 swarm of bees

An adobe village: 2 ostriches

Townhouses: 3 birds

Moscow: 2 phoenixes

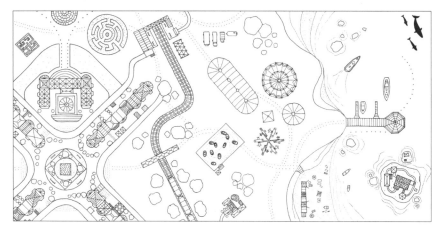

The countryside: 3 whales

High in the clouds: 1 pair of pigeons

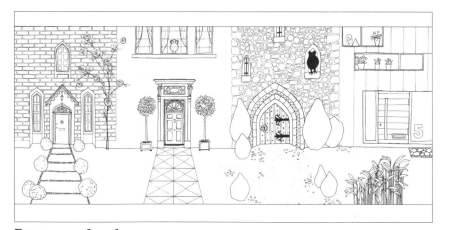

Doorways: 1 owl

An imaginary forest: 1 peacock

Bombay: 1 pigeon

Skyscrapers: 6 butterflies

An imaginary city: 2 sharks

By the sea: 9 fish

A city beneath the waves: 6 jellyfish

Montreal: 2 whales

A treetop city: 5 flying fish

Granada: 6 goldfish

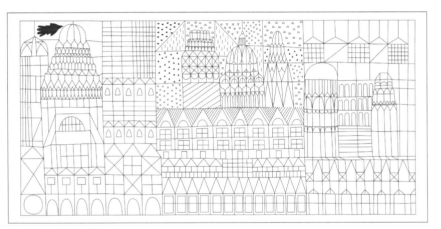

A futuristic city: 1 bird

An imaginary island: 1 bird

London: 2 pigeons

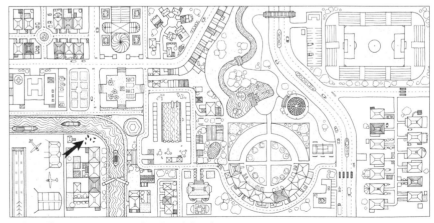

A bird's-eye view: 1 flock of ducks

A city of domes: 1 crow

Istanbul: 1 pack of grouse

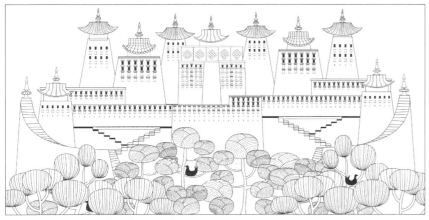

A monastery: 3 birds perching

San Francisco: 3 wrens

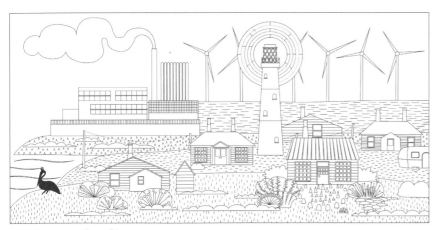

By the sea: 1 pelican

Rio de Janeiro: 1 parrot

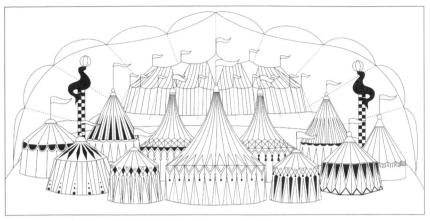

A circus: 2 sea lions

Sydney: 3 bats

Mexico: 2 sparrows

An ice palace: 1 robin

Tokyo: 2 eagles

Jungle: 2 toucans